COUNT IT ALL JOY!

A DEVOTIONAL JOURNEY THROUGH TRIALS

PASTOR JESUS RODRIGUEZ

with
PASTOR NOELIA RODRIGUEZ

ASCEND INTERNATIONAL PUBLISHING

Scripture quotations are from The ESV® Bible (The Holy Bible, English Standard Version®), copyright © 2001 by Crossway, a publishing ministry of Good News Publishers. Used by permission. All rights reserved.

Copyright © 2023 by Jesus Rodriguez All rights reserved. No part of this book may be reproduced, scanned, or distributed in any printed or electronic form without permission.

First Edition: 2023
Printed in the United States of America
Paperback ISBN-13: [978-1-7375059-5-2]

CONTENTS

Introduction   v

Part I
TRIALS AND TRIBULATIONS ARE PART OF OUR JOURNEY IN LIFE, IT IS UP TO US HOW WE REACT.

Day 1: Acknowledging Life's Journey	3
Day 2: Our Response to Trials	6
Day 3: Choosing Joy in Adversity	9
Day 4: Trusting God's Sovereignty	12
Day 5: Growing Through Challenges	15
Day 6: Learning from the Journey	18
Day 7: Responding with Faith, Not Fear	21
Day 8: Cultivating Perseverance	24
Day 9: Transformative Power of Resilience	27
Day 10: Choosing a Positive Perspective	30

Part II
YOU HAVE TO DECIDE TO COUNT IT ALL JOY, NOT A FAÇADE BUT A REVELATION

Day 11: The Decision to Rejoice	35
Day 12: The Authenticity of Joy	38
Day 13: Joy Beyond Circumstances	40
Day 14: The Source of True Joy	42
Day 15: Sharing in Joy and Suffering	45
Day 16: The Revelation of God's Love	47
Day 17: Joy in Surrender	49
Day 18: Joy as a Spiritual Discipline	51
Day 19: Joy in the Midst of Trials	53
Day 20: The Revelation of Eternal Joy	56

Part III
THE REWARD OF PATIENCE AND THE
PROMISE OF NEVER LACKING ANYTHING

Day 21: The Gift of Patience	61
Day 22: Patience in Prayer	63
Day 23: The Fruit of the Spirit: Patience	65
Day 24: Waiting on God's Timing	68
Day 25: Patience in Testing	70
Day 26: Trusting God's Plan	72
Day 27: The Reward of Wisdom through Patience	74
Day 28: Joyful Anticipation	76
Day 29: Patience in Relationships	78
Day 30: Lacking Nothing Through Patience	80
Conclusion	85
Also By the Rodriguez Pastors	87

INTRODUCTION

Welcome to "Counting It All Joy," a devotional series rooted in the wisdom of James 1:2-4. In these verses, James, the brother of Jesus, challenges us to embrace an uncommon perspective toward trials — to not merely endure them but to find genuine joy in the midst of life's challenges.

"Count it all joy, my brothers, when you meet trials of various kinds, for you know that the testing of your faith produces steadfastness. And let steadfastness have its full effect, that you may be perfect and complete, lacking in nothing." (James 1:2-4, ESV)

Throughout the next few days, we will delve into the profound truth that joy can be discovered even in the crucible of trials. Let's embark on this journey together, allowing God's transformative power to shape our understanding of joy and perseverance. May this devotional lead you to a place of deeper faith, resilience, and a joy that surpasses circumstances.

PART I

TRIALS AND TRIBULATIONS ARE PART OF OUR JOURNEY IN LIFE, IT IS UP TO US HOW WE REACT.

DAY 1: ACKNOWLEDGING LIFE'S JOURNEY

Scripture: Psalm 23:4 (ESV)

> *"Even though I walk through the valley of the shadow of death, I will fear no evil, for you are with me; your rod and your staff, they comfort me."*

IF THERE IS something that is sure in life, it is that we are all going to go through some sort of trial or tribulation whether you are a believer or not. Life does not discriminate, whether rich or poor, we will eventually have to face something that will shake us to our core. However, simply because we go through trials and issues, that doesn't mean we are discarded, defeated, counted out or dismissed. There will be times where your default reaction will be feeling upset, sad, frustrated, or irritated. The psalms are filled with David acknowledging the sorrows and hardships of life. In this verse, David emphasizes that even when in the darkest moments of life- even unto death-there is no need to fear. Why? Because David was confident in one very important thing- God has never and would never forsake him. He wrote this psalm from the perspective of a shepherd. Shepherds can never leave their sheep abandoned because they are in constant need of them. God knows we are in constant need of him and promises us to always be with us. Begin this devotional journey by acknowledging that life will be filled with many challenges- many moments that feel incredibly dark, scary and alone. As true as that is, what is even more true is that you will always be comforted by God. A shepherd's rod isn't just used to protect, but also to guide, to correct and to discipline. No matter what the circumstance is, God will bring you comfort and that comfort can take many different forms. Do not fear. He is your Good Shepherd.

REFLECTION QUESTIONS:

How have you been comforted by God in the past?

THE BIBLE SAYS God disciplines those He loves. How has God disciplined you?

. . .

How do you take corrections from your parents? Spouse? Friend? Boss? How can you learn to have a teachable posture when receiving corrections?

DAY 2: OUR RESPONSE TO TRIALS

SCRIPTURE: ROMANS 5:3-4 (ESV)

> "Not only that, but we rejoice in our sufferings, knowing that suffering produces endurance, and endurance produces character, and character produces hope."

ONE COMMON RESPONSE to trials is to find someone to blame. We may begin to think or say "It is my spouse's fault!" "My children are to blame!" If only I made more money- this job doesn't pay me enough!" "My parents messed up!" "It is THEIR fault!" Sometimes, one of these may be true, however, we have to truly understand that although there may be someone to blame, we have to look in the mirror and think "how have I contributed to this?" Society has conditioned us to avoid taking responsibility or to only see things one sided- our side. Some of us are going through the same situations over and over again because we are unable to identify the reality that although we know there is a lesson to learn, we still are looking for a scapegoat to avoid learning a lesson. We must discern and be honest whether what we are facing is a natural consequence of our own sin or it is a trial that is meant ultimately for our good. God has the power to redeem any situation, but we can't put all the blame on him or others when we play a role in the decisions we make as well. It is so important to do a daily examination of our lives.

CONSIDER the Apostle Paul's perspective on suffering. Sometimes we are so focused on the suffering itself that we lose sight of the bigger picture. I remember being at the beach once when the waves were strong. I was standing far enough where the water reached my waist and the waves kept knocking me down. For a moment I was overwhelmed and even grew tired trying to fight my way back to the sand. When I finally made it back to my seat and looked back at the ocean, I saw the line of the horizon far across the ocean. The water looked almost still and yet, I knew there were very strong waves in them.

THIS IS what the apostle Paul is describing. One way we can find joy in the midst of suffering is to focus on what that season will produce- to try and see the situation through God's eyes. There is always an opportunity to grow, to learn and to change. There is a time to mourn, but there is a time for joy. Reflect on how our response to trials can lead to positive outcomes such as endurance, character development, and ultimately, hope.

REFLECTION QUESTIONS:

How can your character change in this season?

WHO IS God transforming you into?

IF YOU ARE NOT SURE, ask the Holy Spirit to help you identify how God is adjusting your character.

DAY 3: CHOOSING JOY IN ADVERSITY

SCRIPTURE: JAMES 1:2-3 (ESV)

"Count it all joy, my brothers, when you meet trials of various kinds, for you know that the testing of your faith produces steadfastness."

It is crucial for us to understand that the Lord uses trials and tribulations to shape us and mold us. If we continue to avoid the shaping and molding, we are going to continue to repeat cycles. Something that was meant to be a day, will last years or even decades. The truth is, trials serve a purpose- to test our faith and produce steadfastness. We must begin to shift our perspective on the problems that we face and instead of seeing them as threats and opposition, we need to start seeing them as opportunities to grow. Sometimes it can feel like what we are going through serves no purpose. Honestly, that will make the circumstance even harder to overcome. The truth is, there is always a purpose in what we are facing. Trials are opportunities to develop our faith and relationship with God. What if instead of complaining and begging God to remove trials, we began to thank God through them? We are not saying this is easy at all, but it is rewarding because it is part of your development as a child of God. We have to change our mindset from a victim mentality of "why me?" to the victor mentality "what needs to mature in my life?"

If we learn to focus on our growth during a trial instead of the suffering, it will bring us closer to experiencing joy in adversity.

I (Noelia) have personal experience of knowing how easy it is to feel overwhelmed and almost paralyzed by the suffering of experiencing adversity. My husband can see me falling into the pit of self-pity and lovingly calls me out when I need a perspective shift. Worship has become one of the ways I help shift my perspective from sadness to thankfulness because it helps consume my mind with the goodness and faithfulness of God. Choosing joy requires intentionality and an active choice to shift your perspective. How can you shift your perspective today?

REFLECTION QUESTIONS:

How are you treating those around you?

How are you using your time and resources?

What choices have you made that you are reaping the consequences for and what trials has God allowed in your life so that you can grow in your faith?

DAY 4: TRUSTING GOD'S SOVEREIGNTY

SCRIPTURE: PROVERBS 3:5-6 (ESV)

> "Trust in the Lord with all your heart, and do not lean on your own understanding. In all your ways acknowledge him, and he will make straight your paths."

Although there is a purpose in every trial that we face, we have to learn that we will not always be able to answer *why* we are facing our struggles. God is sovereign. He created all things and lives outside of our finite time. We cannot understand His mind. But would you want to serve a God who you could fully understand? I want to serve a God who thinks beyond what I can think and can do more than I could even imagine. That is the God that we serve. His ways are not our ways and that is a GOOD thing! Our ways often complicate our paths and create obstacles, while God's ways will make our paths straight. It is usually when we try to be in control that things go array or that we become anxious. Why not choose to trust God in His sovereignty today. You may not get to understand everything, but you can understand that the God of the Universe never leaves you and has your best interest in mind.

This is why the most important part of any trial is using that as an opportunity to learn more about who God is. As humans, it is incredibly difficult to trust someone whom we do not know. Trials are a wonderful opportunity to experience and grow deeper in our understanding of the character of God. To know that God is Jehovah Rapha (Healer) we would have to experience a situation that would require healing. To understand Jehovah Jireh (Provider), we would have to be in a place of need that only God could meet. The truth is, trials help us learn more about God and the more we learn about him, the easier it becomes to trust him and for that to be our default reaction when more trials come in the future. God wants you to get to know him better. He left us the Scriptures, as a way for us to know Him. Increase your daily time in the Word. Make it a priority. Not just because it is something that you should check off your Christian to-do list, but meditate on His Word because it leads to better understanding of who God is and will strengthen your relationship with Him.

REFLECTION QUESTIONS:

What are the areas in your life you find hardest to trust God in? Your children? Spouse? Job? Finances? Dreams?

. . .

Whatever it may be, ask the Holy Spirit to help you surrender these areas to God and trust Him with all of your heart. Joy awaits you on the other side of surrender.

DAY 5: GROWING THROUGH CHALLENGES

SCRIPTURE: 2 CORINTHIANS 4:16-18 (ESV)

> "So we do not lose heart. Though our outer self is wasting away, our inner self is being renewed day by day. For this light momentary affliction is preparing for us an eternal weight of glory beyond all comparison."

In these verses, the Apostle Paul shares profound insights about the intertwining of our earthly struggles and the eternal glory that awaits believers. These words resonate with a call to endurance. Life's challenges may press upon us, but as believers, we are urged not to lose heart. Our faith provides a wellspring of resilience that sustains us amid difficulties. *"Though our outer self is wasting away, our inner self is being renewed day by day."* This paradox unveils a profound spiritual truth. While our physical bodies may experience the wear and tear of life, our inner selves, connected to the eternal, are constantly being renewed by the grace and power of God. In the grand scope of eternity, the challenges we face in this life are described as "light" and "momentary." This perspective invites us to reconsider the weight we assign to our present struggles, knowing they pale in comparison to the glory awaiting us. Here lies the crux of the matter. The trials we endure are not without purpose. Instead, they serve as a refining process, preparing us for a glory so magnificent, it defies comparison. Every struggle becomes a thread woven into the tapestry of our eternal existence.

When the matters of the Kingdom of God outweigh our worries of the world, it becomes so much easier to count it all joy. Balancing full time jobs, pastoring, raising children and the many other hats we carry has not been an easy task. Things can get really hard and ugly. Rather than focusing on the negative situations, we thank God everyday for the privilege of serving him in each of these areas. What a privilege to be parents, to have jobs, and to pastor a church. We have the honor of helping others grow closer to Jesus everyday and we don't take that lightly. The eternal glory that awaits us is so much greater than any hardship we face on this Earth. Meditate on that thought today.

REFLECTIVE QUESTIONS:

How do you typically respond to challenges and trials in your life?

. . .

How does the promise of eternal glory influence your approach to perseverance and endurance?

DAY 6: LEARNING FROM THE JOURNEY

SCRIPTURE: PSALM 119:71 (ESV)

"It is good for me that I was afflicted, that I might learn your statutes."

Trials serve as opportunities for learning and growing in our understanding of God's Word. This proclamation is counterintuitive to our natural inclination to avoid pain and suffering. The psalmist, however, recognizes the goodness found in affliction. It implies that there's inherent value in the trials faced. Affliction is seen as a means of acquiring knowledge and insight into God's statutes—the principles and guidelines found in His Word. The psalmist perceives affliction not as a punishment but as an avenue for spiritual education. These words invite us to view trials as classrooms where God imparts wisdom and understanding. In the midst of adversity, there are lessons to be learned, truths to be grasped, and a deepening of our knowledge of God's character and ways. By saying, *"It is good for me,"* the psalmist turns affliction into a personal testimony. This isn't a theoretical concept but a lived experience. It suggests a profound trust in God's sovereign plan, even when it involves hardship.

So many of us wonder why it is difficult to find joy in the midst of adversity, and the honest truth is that it is because we don't spend enough time in the Word. We want faith that is unshakable, but faith comes through hearing and hearing the word of God (Romans 10:7), therefore, it is impossible to grow in our faith without reading the Word. How can our minds be renewed and how can we have faith in our circumstances, if we aren't spending time getting to know God, know his values and purpose through a vivid study of His Word. If we are honest with ourselves, those of us who struggle being in the Word, have a tendency to open the Bible more when in the middle of a hard situation. If that is the only way you engage with the Word, trials become your only source of growing in your faith. We have to be in the Word as part of our daily rhythm so when trials come we are already prepared to face them.

REFLECTIVE QUESTIONS:

Can you recall a specific instance of affliction that led to a deeper understanding of God's Word?

. . .

IN WHAT WAYS **might challenges provide opportunities for spiritual growth and learning?**

HOW CAN A SHIFT IN PERSPECTIVE—FROM **seeing affliction as purely negative to recognizing its potential for learning—impact your approach to trials?**

DAY 7: RESPONDING WITH FAITH, NOT FEAR

SCRIPTURE: ISAIAH 41:10 (ESV)

> *"Fear not, for I am with you; be not dismayed, for I am your God; I will strengthen you, I will help you, I will uphold you with my righteous right hand."*

God's first reassurance is a call to dispel fear. God says "Do not fear" 365 times in the Bible. The presence of God in our lives is a constant, unchanging reality. In times of trial, He stands beside us, a beacon of strength and comfort. He identifies himself as our God, establishing a personal and intimate connection. This declaration invites us to ground our identity and security in Him rather than being overwhelmed by the challenges we face. God's promise goes beyond mere presence. He actively participates in our situations, providing strength where we feel weak. This assurance instills confidence that, in Him, we find the fortitude needed to endure and overcome. God not only strengthens but extends a helping hand. His assistance is timely, purposeful, and tailored to our needs. The Creator of the universe offers His help to navigate the complexities of our trials. This imagery conveys the idea of God's firm, righteous grip on our lives. His hand upholds, supports, and guides us with unwavering righteousness.

If there is one area God has been actively growing in our family, it is responding with faith and not fear. We have seen testimony after testimony this year of God rescuing, providing, healing and delivering many people out of really scary situations. Fear can be paralyzing and when it consumes us, we are unable to trust God. But we have witnessed people's faith grow through the sharing of testimonies. That is why community is so important to our spiritual growth. We face things so that others who experience similar situations are able to grow in their faith and trust that if God did it before, he can certainly do it again!

REFLECTIVE QUESTIONS:

In what ways do you typically respond to fear and challenges in your life?

How might recognizing God's presence impact your perspective during trials?

. . .

CONSIDER a specific trial you're currently facing. How can God's promise to strengthen, help, and uphold you influence your approach?

DAY 8: CULTIVATING PERSEVERANCE

SCRIPTURE: GALATIANS 6:9 (ESV)

"And let us not grow weary of doing good, for in due season we will reap, if we do not give up."

Paul acknowledges the challenges that may arise in the journey of doing good. The call is to persist in acts of kindness, righteousness, and love even when faced with difficulties. I know personally that this is so much easier to say than to do and Paul is acknowledging that doing good can be demanding. He knew that from experience. He recognizes the reality of human fatigue and the potential for discouragement in the face of challenges. Even so, the promise is one of divine timing. The harvest, the culmination of blessings and rewards, is assured. It may not be immediate, but it will come at the appointed time set by God. It is a Kingdom principle. The condition for reaping the harvest is perseverance. This implies an active choice to endure, to remain steadfast in doing good, and to resist the temptation to succumb to weariness or discouragement.

It always seems like things will come up right when we are in the midst of doing something good for the Kingdom. As we felt called to write this devotional, sickness came into our house and hit us harder than we have ever seen. Even if the sickness doesn't go away as quickly as we would like, we aren't stopping what we have been called to do. These moments require us to depend on the Lord for strength, wisdom and direction. Sometimes we get into such a good rhythm of doing good that we start to do it out of habit or strategy and lose the connection of the Holy Spirit. Dependence on God is an intentional state of being that requires thought, devotion and action. If we don't want to grow weary we HAVE to seek the face of God and rely on the power of the Holy Spirit. There is a battle against the Kingdom of God but we serve a God who has never lost.

REFLECTIVE QUESTIONS:

In what areas of your life do you find it most challenging to persevere in doing good?

CONSIDER a time when you persisted in doing good despite facing challenges. What was the outcome, and how did it impact you?

. . .

How might the assurance of a future harvest influence your mindset when faced with weariness or discouragement?

In what ways can you actively cultivate perseverance in your journey of doing good?

DAY 9: TRANSFORMATIVE POWER OF RESILIENCE

SCRIPTURE: ROMANS 12:12 (ESV)

"Rejoice in hope, be patient in tribulation, be constant in prayer."

The call to rejoice in hope is an invitation to find joy not in current circumstances but in the anticipation of God's promises. Hope becomes an anchor, grounding us amid life's uncertainties. Patience in tribulation requires a steadfast endurance. It's an acknowledgment that challenges are inevitable, but with patience, we can endure and persevere through them. A consistent connection with God through prayer is emphasized. This continual dialogue fosters a deepening relationship, offering guidance, strength, and solace throughout life's journey. The placement of these traits in a single verse suggests their interconnectedness. Hope fuels patience, and both find their strength in constant communion with God through prayer. This triad forms a powerful foundation for resilience.

If we focus too much on the problem and on the past and on what happened to us, we will never be able to receive the new, the good, the blessing, the answer. As a child, I (Jesus) was so excited to try riding my bike without training wheels. I lived at the top of the hill, got on my bike with two wheels and started riding. As I was going down the hill, I looked back to see how far I had gone on just two wheels and was so proud of myself. This moment of excitement was abruptly ended by a loud crash! I slammed right into the fence and busted my lip. This story may seem silly, but it is a perfect illustration of what we tend to do in our lives. It is impossible to walk forward in thankfulness and joy if we are still anchored to the past and have the blinders of complaint on. You can be looking forward but if your vision is trapped in pity, pain, and pettiness, you will not have room for what is new. The Lord does not deposit into bitter people but on people who are thankful. Joy continues to be a choice, a choice of focus! What are you focusing on?

REFLECTIVE QUESTIONS:

Consider a time when you faced a difficult situation. How did hope, patience, and prayer contribute to your resilience?

In what ways can maintaining hope impact your perspective on life's uncertainties?

. . .

How might consistent prayer serve as a source of strength and guidance in the face of challenges?

DAY 10: CHOOSING A POSITIVE PERSPECTIVE

SCRIPTURE: PHILIPPIANS 4:8 (ESV)

> "Finally, brothers, whatever is true, whatever is honorable, whatever is just, whatever is pure, whatever is lovely, whatever is commendable, if there is any excellence, if there is anything worthy of praise, think about these things."

Paul's instruction underscores the significance of our thought life. Our thoughts shape our attitudes, emotions, and actions. Choosing to dwell on positive and virtuous aspects aligns our mindset with God's values. Trials and challenges can often cloud our perspective. However, intentionally focusing on what is good and praiseworthy allows us to discover moments of joy even in difficult circumstances. It becomes a spiritual discipline that uplifts our spirits. A positive perspective doesn't deny the existence of challenges but provides a lens through which we can navigate them. It shapes our response, fostering resilience, hope, and a sense of gratitude even in the midst of adversity. By intentionally choosing what we think about, we guard our hearts against negativity. This doesn't mean ignoring real issues but acknowledging them while also recognizing the goodness that coexists. Focusing on what is true, honorable, just, and praiseworthy aligns our thoughts with the character of God. It's an invitation to participate in God's redemptive narrative and to be agents of hope in the world. As we navigate through our day, let us be intentional about our thought life. May we choose to dwell on the positive, the good, and the praiseworthy. In doing so, we align our hearts with God's perspective, allowing His light to shine even in the darkest moments. Remember, the mind set on what is good is a mind set on God himself, and in his presence, there is fullness of joy.

REFLECTION QUESTIONS:

What dominates your thought life right now?

How does focusing on the positive impact your perspective during trials?

In what ways can you cultivate a more positive thought life?

PART II

YOU HAVE TO DECIDE TO COUNT IT ALL JOY, NOT A FAÇADE BUT A REVELATION

DAY 11: THE DECISION TO REJOICE

SCRIPTURE: PHILIPPIANS 4:4 (ESV)

> *"Rejoice in the Lord always; again, I will say, rejoice."*

I want to start off by reiterating that Joy and Gladness are indeed fruit of the Spirit, but it has to be our decision to express it and live by it. We have to allow the Holy Spirit to dwell inside of our hearts and allow him to teach us how to continuously operate and eat the fruit of Joy daily. We were faced with a difficult situation with someone who was close to us. This person hurt us deeply and we felt betrayed. Even though we gave a lot of ourselves and our resources to them, it didn't stop them from hurting us. This wasn't easy at all but the Lord told us "Rejoice, Count it all Joy and Thank Me for it." We were a little confused but decided to obey and even though we still don't fully understand why everything happened, we chose to be thankful and joyful. When we realize that Joy is not based on what we understand but on Who He is and What He chooses to do, we flow with Him and things work out. In the end, we may get hurt, but our peace and joy cannot be taken from us unless we give someone permission to take it!

This invitation to rejoice is not sporadic or contingent on favorable circumstances; rather, it is a continuous, unwavering response to life's ever-changing situations. The call to rejoice always challenges the notion that joy is dependent on external conditions. Paul's words echo a transcendent joy anchored not in the fleeting nature of circumstances but in the eternal and unchanging nature of the Lord. The repetition emphasizes the importance of this command. It is not merely a suggestion or an option but a divine imperative—an invitation to align our hearts with the source of true and lasting joy. Rejoicing is not just a spontaneous emotion; it's a decision. It's a conscious choice to look beyond challenges, uncertainties, and trials, and to find joy in the abiding presence of the Lord. This decision transforms how we navigate the complexities of life. The foundation of constant joy is the Lord Himself. By rejoicing in Him always, we acknowledge that our joy is sourced in His character, faithfulness, and redemptive work. In every circumstance, His presence remains a wellspring of enduring joy.

REFLECTION QUESTIONS:

What tends to be the primary source of your joy?

. . .

How can you cultivate a mindset of constant rejoicing?

In what ways does constant rejoicing impact your perspective on challenges?

DAY 12: THE AUTHENTICITY OF JOY

SCRIPTURE: PSALM 16:11 (ESV)

> "You make known to me the path of life; in your presence, there is fullness of joy; at your right hand are pleasures forevermore."

This devotional could be summed up with this one verse. If this truth could convict our hearts and minds, joy would be our constant state of being. Psalm 16:11 paints a beautiful picture of the source of true joy—God's presence. Authentic joy is intricately connected to our relationship with Jesus Christ. True joy is found in the discovery and alignment with the path of life that God reveals to us. It goes beyond momentary happiness, offering a profound sense of purpose and direction. This verse unveils the depth of joy that is available in God's presence. It's not a fleeting emotion but a profound and complete joy that encompasses every aspect of our being. The pleasures found in God's presence are not transient; they are eternal. This points to a joy that transcends temporal circumstances, providing an enduring source of delight rooted in the eternal nature of God. True joy is not merely an emotion; it's a fruit of our relationship with God. It blossoms as we walk in alignment with His path, dwell in His presence, and find satisfaction in the eternal pleasures that flow from our connection with Him.

One of the biggest struggles we face is distraction. We are so busy and have so many responsibilities that something so real and constant as the presence of God becomes lost to us. God is always near to us and yet we live like he is not. How can that be? Because we don't take the time to learn how to be in His presence. We aren't talking about proximity, but being truly connected with the living God. Does your schedule revolve around God or do you fit God in whenever you have time leftover? God is always present, we are the ones that need to wake up and become aware of how close He truly is.

REFLECTIVE QUESTIONS:

Where do you currently seek joy in your life?

How has experiencing God's presence impacted your sense of joy?

In what ways can you cultivate a deeper relationship with God for lasting joy?

DAY 13: JOY BEYOND CIRCUMSTANCES

SCRIPTURE: HABAKKUK 3:17-18 (ESV)

> "Though the fig tree should not blossom, nor fruit be on the vines, the produce of the olive fail and the fields yield no food, the flock be cut off from the fold and there be no herd in the stalls, yet I will rejoice in the Lord; I will take joy in the God of my salvation."

Habakkuk paints a vivid picture of barrenness and loss, encompassing a range of agricultural and economic hardships. Despite the dire circumstances described, Habakkuk makes a radical declaration of joy. His joy is not contingent on the prosperity of the land or the abundance of resources but is firmly anchored in his relationship with the Lord. Habakkuk's words emphasize the power of choice. In the face of adversity, he decides to rejoice. This decision underscores the transformative nature of joy—it is an intentional response that can be chosen regardless of external situations. The source of Habakkuk's joy is significant. It is not found in the circumstances themselves but in the unchanging character of the God of his salvation. This points to a joy rooted in the redemptive nature of God, transcending the temporal challenges of life.

One thing that makes hardships so challenging is not knowing their timeline. Sometimes we are going through situations where even knowing it is temporary does not bring us relief. Rather than reasoning our way out of suffering, Habakkuk invites us to shift our perspective completely to something, or rather someone, who is consistent and completely reliable. We should shift our perspective to the nature of God. Even if my circumstances do not change, I am still known, loved, and cared for by the Almighty God. What an incredible honor.

REFLECTIVE QUESTIONS:

What circumstances in your life tend to challenge your joy?

How CAN you cultivate a joy that transcends situations?

IN WHAT WAYS does your relationship with God impact your joy?

DAY 14: THE SOURCE OF TRUE JOY

SCRIPTURE: JOHN 15:11 (ESV)

"These things I have spoken to you, that my joy may be in you, and that your joy may be full."

In John 15:11, Jesus expresses His desire for His joy to be in us, offering the prospect of fullness of joy. Jesus, in His teachings, imparts not just knowledge but a transformative gift—His *own* joy. It is a joy that originates from His divine nature and is offered to dwell within us. He doesn't merely offer a portion of joy but promises fullness. It all begins with his words. Scripture is key to receiving this joy that Jesus promises. We are filled with the joy of the Lord when we are filled with the Holy Spirit! This fullness goes beyond the limitations of earthly circumstances, pointing to a joy that is abundant, complete, and enduring. Reflect on the decision to allow Jesus' joy to reside in us. It's an invitation to open our hearts to His transformative joy, letting it shape our perspectives, emotions, and responses to the challenges of life. Jesus' joy is not contingent on the absence of difficulties but transcends them. It is a resilient, deep-seated joy that remains constant regardless of the ebb and flow of life's circumstances.

To truly grasp this gift of joy that Jesus offers, we have to read what comes before verse 11. In John 15:10 Jesus says, *"If you keep my commandments, you will abide in my love, just as I have kept my Father's commandments and abide in his love. (ESV)"* The key to experiencing the joy Jesus speaks of, is to follow his commandments. Obedience is the pathway to experiencing true joy. He lived as an example during his time on Earth to let us know the power in obedience. So even when hardship comes and you want to quit serving or loving others, remember that it is through our obedience to God that we can receive unlimited joy. There is power in your obedience to God. God sees it and he will reward you for it. Do not give up.

REFLECTIVE QUESTIONS:

How does Jesus' desire for His joy to be in you impact your understanding of joy?

In what ways can you actively invite and nurture Jesus' joy in your daily life?

. . .

How might **His joy empower you to navigate challenges with resilience and hope?**

DAY 15: SHARING IN JOY AND SUFFERING

Scripture: Romans 12:14-16 (ESV)

> "Bless those who persecute you; bless and do not curse them. Rejoice with those who rejoice, weep with those who weep. Live in harmony with one another. Do not be haughty, but associate with the lowly. Never be wise in your own sight."

This is a radical call to respond to persecution with blessings rather than curses. It echoes Jesus' teaching about loving our enemies and reflects a spirit of forgiveness and kindness. We are encouraged to live with empathy and emotional solidarity. It is so easy to simply focus on ourselves when suffering but we must share in the joys and sorrows of others, fostering a sense of community and compassion. Harmony involves unity, understanding, and cooperation. It suggests an intentional effort to maintain peace and goodwill in our relationships, avoiding unnecessary conflicts. This admonition discourages pride and encourages humility. It reminds us to treat everyone with dignity and to avoid looking down on others based on social status or any other external factor. This caution urges against self-righteousness and overconfidence. It encourages a humble recognition of the limitations of our own understanding and the importance of seeking wisdom beyond our perspectives. Our relationship with others should always hold a priority in our lives. Sometimes others can be the source of our suffering and even then God invites us to keep a humble posture. Ask the Holy Spirit to help you see others through the lens that God sees them so you can love them even when you are suffering.

REFLECTIVE QUESTIONS:

How do you typically respond to challenges or mistreatment from others?

In what ways can you actively practice empathy in your relationships?

What steps can you take to avoid self-righteousness and embrace a humble posture?

DAY 16: THE REVELATION OF GOD'S LOVE

SCRIPTURE: ZEPHANIAH 3:17 (ESV)

"The Lord your God is in your midst, a mighty one who will save; he will rejoice over you with gladness; he will quiet you by his love; he will exult over you with loud singing."

This verse begins with the comforting assurance of God's presence. His might is not distant; He is actively involved in the lives of His people, providing salvation and strength. The imagery of God rejoicing over His people with gladness is incredibly intimate and powerful. It paints a picture of a God who takes delight in his creation, finding joy in the relationship with his beloved. God's love has a calming and soothing effect. In the midst of life's storms, His love brings a sense of peace and stillness, providing a refuge where we can find rest and solace. The idea of God singing over His people with loud exultation is a striking image of celebration. It conveys a sense of joy so profound that it bursts forth in exuberant songs of delight.

So often we picture God as a military general or strict parent who only orders people around. How many of us can picture God singing over us or quieting us with his love. This describes a gentle and exciting presence that we don't usually consider. And yet, He is all these things! God *"rejoices over you with gladness"*...let that statement sink in. He is glad, He is happy, he is filled with joy and celebrates with song over YOU! If you haven't smiled yet, you need to keep meditating on this word. God loves you so much. May this thought alone bring you joy today no matter what circumstances you are facing!

REFLECTIVE QUESTIONS:

How does the knowledge of God rejoicing over you impact your understanding of His love?

IN WHAT WAYS have you experienced God's calming love in challenging times?

CONSIDER the joyful image of God singing over you. How might this awareness influence your decision to count it all joy, knowing that you are the object of His delight?

DAY 17: JOY IN SURRENDER

SCRIPTURE: GALATIANS 2:20 (ESV)

"I have been crucified with Christ. It is no longer I who live, but Christ who lives in me. And the life I now live in the flesh I live by faith in the Son of God, who loved me and gave himself for me."

The journey of joy begins with surrender. Paul acknowledges that his old self, with its selfish desires and pursuits, has been crucified. This act of surrender is the starting point for a new life in Christ. Surrender can feel scary because we get so used to holding on to things that we can't imagine letting go and feeling empty. But surrender is not an emptying without purpose. It is an invitation for Christ to take residence within us. Joy is found in the realization that our lives are now infused with the presence and power of Christ himself. The Christian life is a journey of faith—a continuous reliance on the Son of God. Joy is discovered in the trust that, despite our weaknesses, Christ's life and strength sustain us. The foundation of our surrender and subsequent joy is rooted in Christ's love and sacrificial act. His love becomes the wellspring of joy, reminding us of the depth of His commitment and grace.

Biblical joy is a response to the good news of Jesus. Trials are good news because we are being developed into the image of Christ and how we react will determine how quickly we will be able to exit the trial. Joy in a trail is not a facade but a revelation. Knowing that through it all, God will be glorified!

REFLECTIVE QUESTIONS:

Consider your understanding of surrender. How might surrendering your desires, plans, and self-will align with the crucifixion of the old self mentioned in this verse?

Reflect on moments when you sensed the presence of Christ in your life. How did His indwelling bring about a sense of joy, peace, or fulfillment?

Reflect on the love and sacrifice of Christ. How might a deep awareness of His love for you inspire joy as you yield to His lordship and allow Him to live through you?

DAY 18: JOY AS A SPIRITUAL DISCIPLINE

SCRIPTURE: PSALM 118:24 (ESV)

> *"This is the day that the Lord has made; let us rejoice and be glad in it."*

Every day is a creation of the Lord. There's intentionality in every sunrise, and every moment is under the divine sovereignty of our Creator. There is an invitation in this Scripture—a call to actively engage in the spiritual discipline of rejoicing. It's not a passive response but a deliberate decision to find joy in the midst of whatever the day may hold. Rejoicing is not merely an emotional response; it's a spiritual discipline. It involves training our minds and hearts to see God's goodness and faithfulness, even in challenging circumstances. It's a choice to focus on His sovereignty rather than on our circumstances. Each day presents a choice—to grumble or to rejoice. Choosing joy intentionally is a transformative decision that shifts our perspective. It involves cultivating a grateful heart and recognizing the countless blessings that surround us, even in the mundane.

So just how do we do this? Scripture helps us by telling us that we must take every thought captive to the obedience of Christ (2 Corinthians 10:5 ESV) and replace these negative thoughts and lies with truth that Jesus has revealed to us. Ignoring the thoughts is not enough, you have to actively reject them and replace them. This is how you train your brain to live in a state of gratitude. Anxiety and gratitude cannot coexist in your brain. This is why God is constantly inviting us to cast our worries on him and to be thankful and to rejoice because he knows what it takes for us to be free no matter the challenges we face. This does not mean you ignore the reality of your situation, it means you highlight the reality of the goodness of God more than your situation.

REFLECTIVE QUESTIONS:

How do you typically approach the start of a new day?

CONSIDER **a recent day when challenges seemed overwhelming. How might the discipline of rejoicing have influenced your perspective?**

HOW MIGHT REJOICING **as a spiritual discipline impact your relationship with God and others?**

DAY 19: JOY IN THE MIDST OF TRIALS

SCRIPTURE: *2 CORINTHIANS 7:4 (ESV)*

> *"I am acting with great boldness toward you; I have great pride in you; I am filled with comfort. In all our affliction, I am overflowing with joy."*

Despite facing challenges and affliction, Paul displays a sense of boldness. His actions are not fueled by fear or despair but by a confidence that transcends circumstances. Paul's pride isn't rooted in arrogance but in a deep sense of connection with the Corinthian believers. Even in their challenges, he finds reasons to be proud, revealing a joy that stems from witnessing spiritual growth. His focus goes beyond the things of this world. His joy is rooted in the Kingdom of God. Seeing others grow closer to Jesus fills him with joy even when he is experiencing the worst pain and suffering. In the midst of affliction, Paul experiences profound comfort. This comfort is not a fleeting emotion but a deep assurance that comes from his unwavering trust in God's sovereignty. Perhaps the most striking statement—Paul's joy isn't diminished by affliction; it overflows. This is a joy that defies circumstances, rooted in the eternal perspective of God's redemptive plan.

It is important to remember what the Psalmist said *"Many are the afflictions of the righteous, but the Lord delivers him out of them all. (Psalm 34:19, ESV)"* There is a promise that the Lord will deliver you from all of your trials, they are not eternal. Choose to thank God even when it doesn't make sense. Let's look at Paul and Silas as examples. They were imprisoned for rebuking a spirit of divination (Acts 16). They were beaten and thrown into the deepest cell in jail. They had every right to be angry, frustrated, hurt, and questioning their call in the Lord and yet they chose joy. What did they do? They prayed and worshiped God even if others were listening. People will always be looking to see how we respond to situations. What sets us apart as Christians is how we respond to circumstances. Ultimately, the Lord delivered Paul and Silas and through them a man received salvation that night. There is power in your worship. Choose to worship God even when your circumstances make you want to stay quiet or just complain. Worship helps us focus on the goodness and faithfulness of God which will help us to live in a state of joy.

REFLECTIVE QUESTIONS:

Does witnessing spiritual growth in others fill you with joy the way it did Paul?

. . .

DAY 19: JOY IN THE MIDST OF TRIALS | 55

CONSIDER a specific trial you are currently facing. How might Paul's example influence your perspective on joy in the midst of affliction?

How CAN your perspective shift from the things of this world to the Kingdom of God?

DAY 20: THE REVELATION OF ETERNAL JOY

SCRIPTURE: REVELATION 21:4 (ESV)

"He will wipe away every tear from their eyes, and death shall be no more, neither shall there be mourning, nor crying, nor pain anymore, for the former things have passed away."

God promises that He will wipe away every tear, and there will be no more death, mourning, crying, or pain—an assurance that shapes our decision to count it all joy as a reflection of the eternal joy promised by God. Have you ever had someone wipe away your tears or wiped away the tears of a child? The imagery of God personally wiping away tears conveys an intimate act of comfort. This gesture represents the complete eradication of sorrow and distress. God could have said "you will no longer cry" but instead He chooses to phrase it in a way that shows how personal and close He is-close enough to wipe away your tears. In eternity, the sting of death is forever removed. The absence of mourning signifies a state where the causes of grief and loss are eradicated. The promise of a new heaven and a new earth signals a complete transformation. Everything associated with the fallen state of the world—suffering, sin, and death—will be replaced with God's perfect order. This is what we have to look forward to! Do not lose hope!

REFLECTIVE QUESTIONS:

How does the promise of Revelation 21:4 impact your perspective on the trials and challenges you face in the present?

Consider a time when you experienced deep sorrow or pain. How might the assurance of God wiping away every tear influence your understanding of that experience?

In what ways can the anticipation of eternal joy shape your decision to count it all joy in your current circumstances?

PART III

THE REWARD OF PATIENCE AND THE PROMISE OF NEVER LACKING ANYTHING

DAY 21: THE GIFT OF PATIENCE

S<small>CRIPTURE</small>: J<small>AMES</small> *5:7-8 (ESV)*

> *"Be patient, therefore, brothers, until the coming of the Lord. See how the farmer waits for the precious fruit of the earth, being patient about it, until it receives the early and the late rains. You also, be patient. Establish your hearts, for the coming of the Lord is at hand."*

In James 5:7-8, the analogy of a farmer patiently waiting for the harvest provides a rich metaphor for understanding the gift of patience and its connection to the rewards to come. The farmer exemplifies patience in the agricultural process. Patiently awaiting the necessary rains and allowing the crops to grow and mature reflects the virtue of patience. James extends the analogy to the believers, encouraging them to embody the same patience. Patience is presented as a virtue, a quality that allows for growth, development, and the fulfillment of God's promises in due time. Patience involves more than just waiting; it requires a firm and steadfast heart. The call to establish the heart suggests the intentional cultivation of patience as a foundational aspect of one's character. The ultimate reward is the coming of the Lord. The analogy reminds believers that, like the awaited harvest, there is an appointed time for the fulfillment of God's promises and the arrival of the Lord.

REFLECTIVE QUESTIONS:

Consider the stages of a harvest. How might the process of waiting for the early and late rains parallel seasons of waiting and patience in your life?

Reflect on specific situations where patience is required. How might embracing the virtue of patience positively impact your perspective and approach in these areas?

Consider the idea of establishing your heart. How can you intentionally cultivate patience as a foundational aspect of your character, especially in light of the imminent reward mentioned in the passage?

DAY 22: PATIENCE IN PRAYER

SCRIPTURE: PSALM 40:1 (ESV)

> *"I waited patiently for the Lord; he inclined to me and heard my cry."*

There is a beautiful connection between patience and prayer. The psalmist's choice to wait patiently suggests an intentional and enduring commitment to trust in God's timing. Patience in waiting becomes an active expression of faith and reliance on God. God inclines his ear to our prayers. The God of the Universe draws close to us and gives us His full attention. He is not like the rigid and lifeless statues that many worshiped throughout history, but he is a personal God that literally moves on our behalf. Our struggle sometimes lies in what we worship or who we pray to. Do we go to God in prayer or to our friends, coworkers, social media, or other outlets before we go to Jesus? Many times we feel hopeless because we create idols that are unable to provide the life and hope that only Jesus can provide. Patience in waiting and persistent prayer go hand in hand. Patient waiting is not passive but an active expression of trust and dependence on the living God! It aligns with persistent, heartfelt prayers that acknowledge God's sovereignty and wisdom. God doesn't only draw near to us to listen to our cries but he also gives a timely response. God hears the cry of the patient heart and acts in accordance with his perfect timing.

REFLECTIVE QUESTIONS:

Reflect on past experiences where God inclined toward you and heard your cry. How did God's attentive response reinforce your trust in Him?

Consider the dynamic between patience in waiting and persistent prayer. How do these two aspects of faith work together to deepen your dependence on God?

In what ways can you cultivate patience in your prayer life?

DAY 23: THE FRUIT OF THE SPIRIT: PATIENCE

SCRIPTURE: GALATIANS 5:22-23 (ESV)

> *"But the fruit of the Spirit is love, joy, peace, patience, kindness, goodness, faithfulness, gentleness, self-control; against such things, there is no law."*

Patience is not a product of human effort but a fruit that naturally grows in the life of a person who is yielded to the Holy Spirit. It is a divine quality infused by the Spirit into the believer's character. The presence of patience in our lives is an indication that the Spirit is at work within us. It is a virtue that develops as we surrender to the transformative work of the Holy Spirit, allowing Him to shape our attitudes and responses. The fruit of patience is part of a larger tapestry of virtues that characterize a Spirit-filled life. It exists in harmony with love, joy, peace, kindness, goodness, faithfulness, gentleness, and self-control. Together, these fruits reflect the multifaceted nature of God's character. The virtues listed, including patience, stand in contrast to the legalistic approach of trying to earn righteousness through adherence to rules. The Spirit produces these qualities organically, fostering a life guided by love and grace.

The reason we need the Holy Spirit to develop patience within us is because patience is a characteristic of God. The more we get to know the character of God, the more we will be able to develop the fruit of patience. *"The Lord is merciful and gracious, slow to anger and abounding in steadfast love.* (Psalm 103:8, ESV)" Patience means to suffer long and goes hand-in-hand with mercy. To understand the patience of God, read the story of the Prodigal Son from the perspective of the Father (Luke 15). A Father who was rejected and dishonored by his son, waited for his son to return day after day. He knew his son was suffering and yet longed for him to be home with him. When the son finally came to his senses and returned home, the Father saw him from afar and ran to him. You know what this tells me? Everyday, the Father went outside to see if the son had returned. And everyday the son did not return was another day full of suffering and sadness for the Father. Patience requires suffering but it will always lead to a season of joy. The Father had every right to be bitter for the suffering his son put him through, but instead, the Father rejoiced at his return! That is how our Heavenly Father is, he is patient with us and merciful. He chooses to love us even when we don't deserve it. What a wonderful Father we have and an example of true patience.

REFLECTIVE QUESTIONS:

In what ways do you see patience as a reflection of the Spirit's work in your life?

How does cultivating patience align with your surrender to the Spirit's guidance?

In what areas of your life can you intentionally invite the Spirit to cultivate more patience?

DAY 24: WAITING ON GOD'S TIMING

SCRIPTURE: ECCLESIASTES 3:1 (ESV)

> "For everything there is a season, and a time for every matter under heaven."

Every event, circumstance, and season has its appointed time in the divine order of things. There is a purposeful unfolding of events orchestrated by God, and each has its proper time. The concept of divine timing inherently calls for patience. It acknowledges that certain matters and seasons have their designated moments. Waiting patiently involves trusting in God's wisdom and sovereignty over the unfolding of our lives. Waiting for God's perfect timing requires trusting His wisdom. It acknowledges that God sees the bigger picture and understands the intricate details of our lives. The rewards come not just in the fulfillment of desires but in the growth of our trust and faith in Him.

There is a unique beauty in aligning our lives with God's timing. It allows us to witness the manifestation of His plans and experience the richness of His blessings at precisely the right moments.

The unknown of time is always a factor that makes trials harder to endure. Rather than continuously asking "how long will this last?" or asking other questions that do not bring any answers, focus on asking the right questions. Ask questions like, "how can I learn from this?", "what is God trying to teach me?", "who will I share this testimony with to bless their faith and bring them hope?". These questions help you to accept the timing of God and recognize that his plan is greater than anything you can come up with on your own. Choose to trust him.

REFLECTIVE QUESTIONS:

In what areas of your life have you experienced the concept of divine timing?

How does the acknowledgment of divine timing impact your perspective on patience?

What challenges do you face in waiting for God's timing, and how can you navigate them?

DAY 25: PATIENCE IN TESTING

SCRIPTURE: ROMANS 8:18 (ESV)

"For I consider that the sufferings of this present time are not worth comparing with the glory that is to be revealed to us"

We need to consider, or weigh, our present sufferings so we can gain a perspective that acknowledges the temporary nature and limitations of current trials. The suffering of this present time is deemed as not worth comparing with the future glory. This comparison highlights the vast difference between the challenges we face now and the unparalleled glory that God promises to reveal to His people. The use of the term "to be revealed to us" emphasizes the certainty of the future glory. It is not a vague or uncertain hope but a promise grounded in the character and faithfulness of God.

We are not able to comprehend the glory that is awaiting

us. We are so used to the suffering in this world, that it is hard to picture the complete eradication of all these things once we reach heaven. We receive glimpses of glory during our time on Earth through worship and fellowship with our brothers and sisters in Christ. Notice those moments where all you feel is joy and connection with Jesus and his people. The glory of God is manifested while we are still on Earth. He uses trials to bring us from one level of glory to the next. He is preparing us for what is to come- an incomparable glory in his eternal presence!

REFLECTIVE QUESTIONS:

How does this verse influence your perspective on present sufferings?

IN WHAT WAYS **can a focus on future glory impact your endurance through trials?**

REFLECT ON A TIME **when the hope of future glory sustained you through a difficult season.**

DAY 26: TRUSTING GOD'S PLAN

SCRIPTURE: *1 PETER 1:6-7 (ESV)*

> *In this you rejoice, though now for a little while, if necessary, you have been grieved by various trials, so that the tested genuineness of your faith —more precious than gold that perishes though it is tested by fire—may be found to result in praise and glory and honor at the revelation of Jesus Christ."*

In the journey of faith, trials are not an absence of joy but a pathway to a deeper, more resilient joy. In 1 Peter 1:6-7 (ESV), Peter acknowledges the reality of various trials that may bring temporary grief. Yet, he unveils a profound truth: these trials serve as a refining fire for our faith, much like gold being tested in the fire. Consider the analogy of gold. Gold, though precious, is purified and strengthened through the intense heat of the refining process. Similarly, our faith, when tested by the fires of trials, becomes more genuine, enduring, and valuable. This process is not without purpose; it is designed to lead us to a place of praise, glory, and honor when Christ is revealed. So, in the midst of trials, rejoice not only in the immediate, tangible joys but also in the unseen work of refinement happening within. Your faith, proven genuine through trials, is a treasure more precious than gold. As you face challenges, hold onto the hope that the outcome will be a praise-filled life that brings glory and honor to the One who refines and reveals.

REFLECTION QUESTIONS:

How do you typically view trials in your life—merely as obstacles or as opportunities for faith refinement?

In what ways have you experienced the tested genuineness of your faith through trials?

How can the knowledge that your faith is more precious than gold influence your response to current trials?

What steps can you take to cultivate a mindset of rejoicing in trials, trusting in the refining work of God?

DAY 27: THE REWARD OF WISDOM THROUGH PATIENCE

SCRIPTURE: JAMES 1:5 (ESV)

> *"If any of you lacks wisdom, let him ask God, who gives generously to all without reproach, and it will be given him."*

In the journey of life, wisdom is a precious guide, illuminating the path we walk. James 1:5 (ESV) extends an open invitation to seek wisdom from God, the giver of all good things. It's an invitation that stands regardless of our circumstances, doubts, or shortcomings. If we lack wisdom, we are encouraged to ask, and God, in His generosity, promises to bestow it upon us without reproach.

God does not withhold wisdom from His children but offers it abundantly. As we navigate the complexities of life, uncertain of the next steps, His wisdom becomes a reliable compass. This divine wisdom is not rationed or hesitant; it is given generously, overflowing with insights that lead to discernment, understanding, and righteous choices.

So, in the moments of confusion, decisions, or the unknown, let's approach the throne of grace with confidence, asking for the wisdom that God, in His abundant love, longs to impart. Counting it all joy is a decision, when we do, our faith helps us push through and the Lord will reward us. Wisdom is a reward that awaits us when we ask.

REFLECTION QUESTIONS:

In what areas of your life do you currently seek wisdom?

WHAT DOES it mean for you personally to ask God for wisdom "without reproach"?

HOW HAVE you experienced the generosity of God in providing wisdom in the past?

IN WHAT WAYS can you actively cultivate a habit of seeking God's wisdom in your daily life?

DAY 28: JOYFUL ANTICIPATION

SCRIPTURE: ROMANS 8:25 (ESV)

"But if we hope for what we do not see, we wait for it with patience."

In Romans 8:25 (ESV), we are reminded that true hope goes hand in hand with patience. As we hope for what lies beyond our current sight, whether it be dreams, promises, or the fulfillment of God's plans, we are called to wait with patient expectation. Imagine a garden in winter, where beneath the frost and snow, life stirs, preparing for the bloom that is yet unseen. Similarly, our hopes, when rooted in God, hold the promise of a future unseen but deeply anticipated. The waiting is not passive; it's a journey of patient trust in the One who orchestrates the unfolding of time. The hope we have is like an expecting mother. As the baby grows in her womb, she awaits with great expectation the eventual birth. And yet, the mother is already connected to the child, the baby can hear the mother's voice and feel her heartbeat. This is a picture of the already-but-not-yet. What we hope might not be in view yet, but we wait for it with patience knowing it will come. Hope is not aimlessly waiting for something to arrive, but an assurance of what we have yet to see coming to pass.

So, as you hold onto your hopes, be reminded that the wait is not in vain. With each passing day, with each season of anticipation, God is at work, bringing to fruition that which you hope for, even if it's beyond your current view.

REFLECTION QUESTIONS:

What are some things you are currently hoping for or anticipating in your life?

How do you typically approach waiting for the fulfillment of your hopes?

In what ways does the connection between hope and patience deepen your trust in God's timing?

What can you do to cultivate patience while waiting for the fulfillment of your hopes?

DAY 29: PATIENCE IN RELATIONSHIPS

SCRIPTURE: COLOSSIANS 3:12 (ESV)

"Put on then, as God's chosen ones, holy and beloved, compassionate hearts, kindness, humility, meekness, and patience."

In Colossians 3:12 (ESV), we are given a wardrobe of virtues to put on as God's chosen and beloved ones. It's a divine attire, woven with compassion, kindness, humility, meekness, and patience. Each piece is not just a garment but an embodiment of our identity in Christ. Imagine adorning yourself with compassion, wrapping kindness around you, wearing the cloak of humility, the gentle attire of meekness, and the enduring fabric of patience. Patience is the outer cloak that allows you to develop in the fullness of the character of Christ. Our character develops through trials, so therefore, without patience, we would give up before we are able to grow in compassion, kindness and meekness. As you intentionally put on these virtues, you're not just dressing; you're stepping into the character of Christ.

So, today, let your attire be more than what meets the eye. Let it be a reflection of the transformative work God is doing within you—a living testament to His chosen, holy, and beloved ones.

REFLECTION QUESTIONS:

Which of these virtues—compassion, kindness, humility, meekness, and patience—resonates with you the most at this moment?

How does the idea of putting on these virtues align with your understanding of your identity as God's chosen and beloved?

In what situations or relationships can you actively put on one or more of these virtues today?

DAY 30: LACKING NOTHING THROUGH PATIENCE

Scripture: James 1:4 (ESV)

> *"And let steadfastness have its full effect, that you may be perfect and complete, lacking in nothing."*

In the crucible of challenges, there is a refining work happening within us. James 1:4 (ESV) beckons us to let steadfastness—the unwavering endurance in the face of trials—have its full effect. It's not just enduring for the sake of endurance but allowing this steadfastness to mold and shape us until we become perfect and complete, lacking in nothing.

Imagine a tree weathering the seasons. The steadfastness with which its roots hold firm in storms allows it to grow deeper and stronger. Similarly, as we navigate life's storms with unwavering endurance, we are being perfected and completed, rooted in a resilience that leads to a lack of nothing.

So, today, let your steadfastness be more than survival. Let it be a transformative journey, shaping you into the person God envisions—a masterpiece of endurance, lacking nothing.

So we arrive at a crucial decision point-choosing joy. It is not a denial of challenges but an affirmation of faith. In the face of trials, we have the power to choose joy, a joy that emanates from a deep relationship with our Lord. What you are unable to conquer or embrace the lesson or the molding, will be left over for your children or grandchildren to manage. Lacking nothing is not just a promise for you, but for your generations to come. Wouldn't it be better to embrace the molding now and count it all joy than to see your generation go through your trial because we refused to center ourselves in Jesus. What we refuse to learn becomes a stumbling block for the next generation, but what we choose to overcome with joy and patience, becomes a stepping stone for them!

REFLECTION QUESTIONS:

What challenges or trials are currently testing your steadfastness?

How DO you typically respond to challenges—merely enduring or intentionally allowing them to refine you?

. . .

IN WHAT WAYS can you actively let steadfastness have its full effect in your current circumstances?

CONCLUSION

As we conclude this 30-day journey of "Counting It All Joy," we've explored the profound wisdom of James 1:2-4, discovering that joy is not a fleeting emotion but a steadfast choice rooted in the character of God. Through trials and tribulations, we've learned to let joy permeate our hearts, not as a facade but as a revelation of our faith.

In each devotional entry, we delved into the transformative power of joy, understanding that it is intricately connected to our relationship with Jesus. We explored the rewards of patience, the impact of resilience, and the eternal perspective that anchors our joy.

As we step away from these 30 days, may the practice of counting it all joy become more than a habit—it should be a lifestyle. Let joy be the melody that accompanies you through every trial, the strength that sustains you in challenges, and the revelation that transforms your perspective.

May you continue to count it all joy, not just in moments

of ease but especially in the crucible of trials. For in choosing joy, you align yourself with the promises of God, embracing the completeness and maturity that come from trusting Him through every season.

May your journey be marked by unwavering joy, deepening faith, and a profound sense of God's presence in all things. Count it all joy, dear friend, for you are held in the embrace of a joy-giving God.

With joyous blessings,

Jesus and Noelia Rodriguez

"May the God of hope fill you with all joy and peace in believing, so that by the power of the Holy Spirit you may abound in hope" - Romans 15:13

ALSO BY THE RODRIGUEZ PASTORS

A MOTHER'S
Devotion

NOELIA RODRIGUEZ

Made in the USA
Middletown, DE
03 January 2024